Christy's Mystery...Clues From The Hidden
By Anne T. Garcia

Printed in the United States of America

Scripture quotation taken from the
New King James Version

Waymaker Publishers
P.O. Box 1481
Fenton, MO 63026
waymaker@sbcglobal.net
1.866.618.2609

Illustrations and Cover design
by Keith R. and Donna F. Cherry

A special thank you to Dan Lennox of
Hidden Entertainment; Hollywood, CA
for being "Daddy" in the illustration on page 19.

Christy's Mystery...

Clues From The Hidden

by Anne T. Garcia

Dedication

This book is Dedicated

With great love

And deep affection

To (in Hebrew), Mishpahati,

Our Families

This Book Belongs To

Arweh.

Given By

ERiePAPA

This Date

4 - 5 - 1 2

"Behold children are a heritage from the Lord."
Psalm 127:3

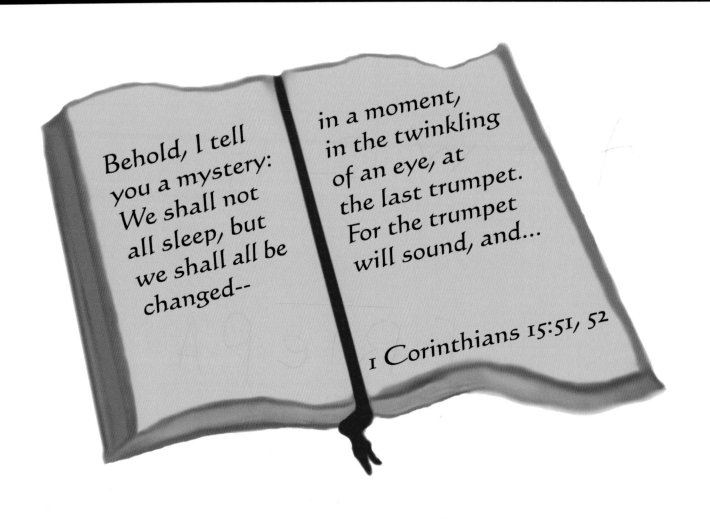

Behold, I tell you a mystery: We shall not all sleep, but we shall all be changed--

in a moment, in the twinkling of an eye, at the last trumpet. For the trumpet will sound, and...

1 Corinthians 15:51, 52

The mystery unfolds within these pages. Read and see what Christy discovered with clues From The Hidden!

On Christmas night, everyone went to Grandma's house for dinner. Grandma used her nice dishes and new table cloth. Opened gifts were piled high, and torn wrapping paper had been stuffed in a big plastic bag and thrown away. Everybody had gotten up early this morning to open presents.

After dinner the grown ups said, "Grandma, you rest. We'll do the dishes."

1

Grandma walked into the family room and sank into the sofa. She stared at the manger scene she had placed on the table near the fireplace. She looked at the little statues of Jesus, Mary and Joseph in the stable. They told the story of the first Christmas day.

Christy, age eight, walked over to Grandma and sat down, too. "What are you thinking about Grandma?" she asked.

"Oh, I'm just thinking that Jesus was born a long time ago and how even our calendar marks time from Jesus' birth," Grandma replied.

"Really?" inquired Christy, who was pretty smart for eight years old.

"Does that mean Jesus was born more than 2,000 years ago?"

"That's right, dear," Grandma answered with a smile.

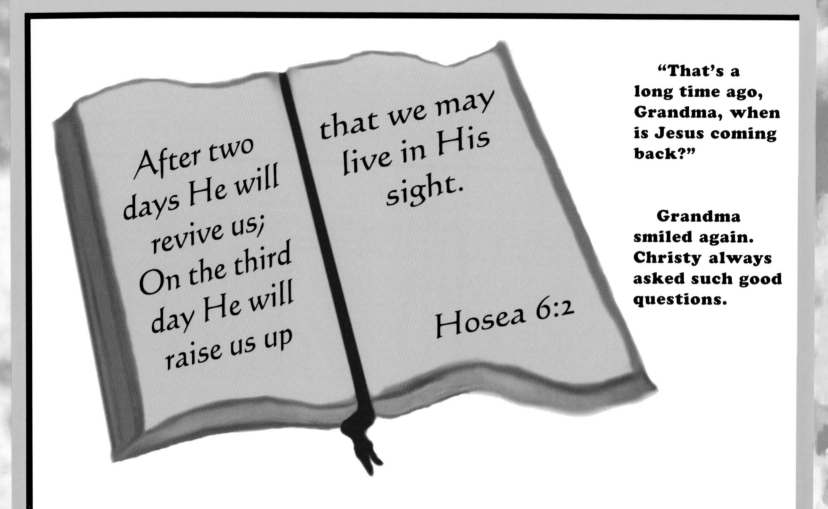

After two days He will revive us;
On the third day He will raise us up
that we may live in His sight.

Hosea 6:2

"That's a long time ago, Grandma, when is Jesus coming back?"

Grandma smiled again. Christy always asked such good questions.

She answered thoughtfully, "Jesus is coming back very soon Christy, before you and your brothers grow up. That's what it says in the Bible."

"Before I grow up?" asked Christy. Christy was surprised. "Where does it say that in the Bible?" she asked in a very loud voice.

Grandma opened the Bible and read Hosea 6:2. (Read Hosea 6:2)

"I know, I know," exclaimed Christy happily. "I'll bet 'on the third day He will raise us up...' means the Rapture. Pastor Willie said we will go to heaven in the Rapture."

"But Grandma," she said after she thought about it some more, "That says after two days. You said Jesus lived 2,000 years ago."

Suddenly Christy realized it didn't quite make sense.

Grandma knew what Christy was thinking.

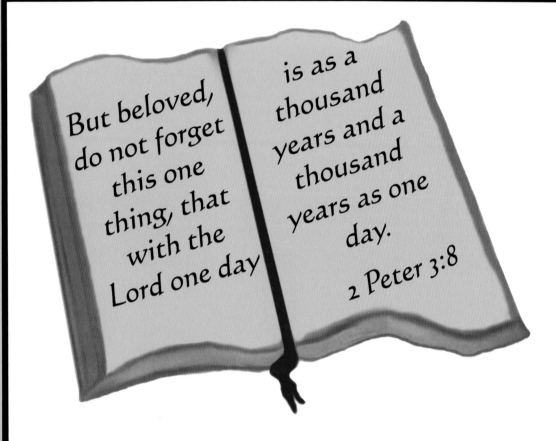

But beloved, do not forget this one thing, that with the Lord one day is as a thousand years and a thousand years as one day.

2 Peter 3:8

"Remember dear, we have to take all the verses in the Bible and put them together, like a puzzle, to understand it."

Grandma got her Bible and began to read 2 Peter 3:8 to make the picture clear. (Read 2 Peter 3:8)

Christy wrinkled her nose, "What does 'one day is as a thousand years' mean Grandma?"

Grandma answered, "That means when one day goes by in heaven, a thousand years go by on earth."

"How can that be, Grandma?" Christy asked. Christy really didn't understand it at all.

"Albert Einstein was a very smart man who lived a long time ago and he understood science better than anybody. We still study his teachings today and he explained that time is just a dimension," Grandma said.

"What's a dimension, Grandma?" Christy asked. Grandma tried to explain.

"Let's go look at your goldfish swimming in his bowl, Christy. He can swim up or down, back and forth. That's because his bowl has length, it has width and it has height. You can pick his bowl up and move it and it doesn't affect your fish at all. You are outside of that fishbowl and you control it."

"Our world is like God's fishbowl. He is outside of time, and He controls our future. God promised that about 2,000 years after Jesus' birth, Jesus would return and clean up the mess made by sin.

His Church will go to heaven before He cleans up the mess."

"Why didn't Jesus give us more clues so we could understand it better?" Christy wondered. "He gave us lots and lots of clues," Grandma explained. "That's why I wrote a book for grown ups to read. I wanted to explain the clues."

Christy ran over and picked up the book, <u>From the Hidden</u> from the coffee table. "This book Grandma?" she asked, holding the book in her hands as she sat down. "The one with the world in an hourglass on the cover?"

"That's the one," answered Grandma. Grandma sat back down too.

"Tell me another clue, one you wrote about in this book," Christy pleaded.

ISRAEL

"Well," said Grandma, "the biggest clue of all was a fig tree."

"What does that mean?" asked Christy.

"When the apostles asked Jesus when He would return, He said to watch the fig tree," Grandma explained.

"The fig tree stands for a tiny little country in the Middle East, far away. The fig tree is Israel, the homeland of the Jews."

"Mommy and Daddy pray for the Jews all the time," said Christy, remembering how Daddy leads family prayer. "Only they don't call them Israel, they call them 'Jim Ruselem'."

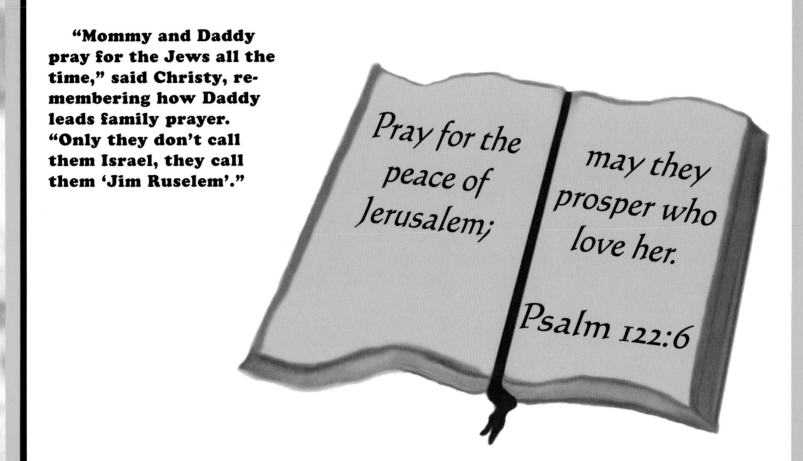

Pray for the peace of Jerusalem; may they prosper who love her.

Psalm 122:6

"No, Christy, that's 'Jerusalem'," Grandma corrected her softly.

"That's right, I remember now, 'Pray for the peace of Jerusalem.' (Read Psalm 122:6) But Grandma," Christy inquired, "Why does God want us to pray for a country so far away?"

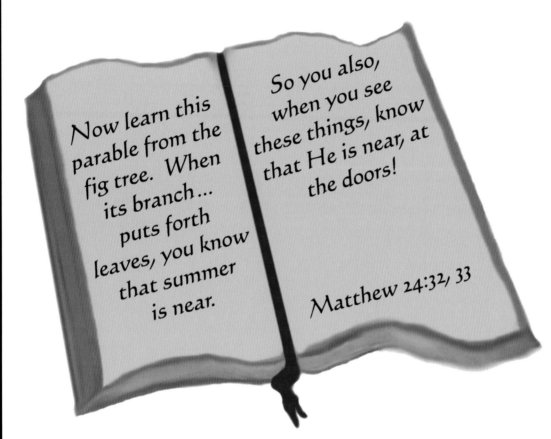

Now learn this parable from the fig tree. When its branch... puts forth leaves, you know that summer is near.

So you also, when you see these things, know that He is near, at the doors!

Matthew 24:32, 33

"Israel is God's time clock, darling," Grandma answered. "God said the generation that saw Israel become a nation again would still be here when Jesus returns for His church after 2,000 years. (Read Matthew 24:32, 33) Israel became a nation on May 14, 1948."

"1948? That was a long time ago. The people who lived then are probably all dead by now," said Christy, trying to sound very smart.

"I was alive in 1948," said Grandma, with a big smile spreading across her face. Christy didn't answer.

After some cookies and hot chocolate, Grandma took Christy's hand and walked her to the guest bedroom. Christy liked to spend the night at Grandma's. She missed Mommy, Daddy and the boys a little bit. Still, she felt really grown up because she was old enough to spend the night.

She crawled into bed before she said her prayers. It had started snowing outside and it was too cold to kneel down. Pastor Willie had taught her that it's always nice to pray before you go to sleep.

Christy had gone to Pastor Willie's church ever since she could remember. She knew that Jesus would come very soon, and all the children would go up to meet Jesus in the clouds. Pastor Willie had said so many times.

Of course, lots of grown ups will go up to meet Jesus, too. Everybody who wants to go can go; everybody who loves Jesus, that is.

Pastor Willie invited people who wanted to love Jesus to come down to the altar at church, almost every week.

Grandma covered Christy with a goose down comforter and kissed her
goodnight. While Christy was thinking about how warm and snuggly she felt,
she fell fast asleep.

Christy had a dream. In the dream, it was her brother Raymond's birthday.

He was born in September.

There was a big party, and all the family was at her house.

All her aunts and uncles, cousins and friends were there. Everyone was laughing and having a wonderful time. They had a fried chicken dinner and a cake decorated at the grocery store.

Suddenly, in Christy's dream, there was a great SWOOSHING sound. Christy was going through the roof of the house! Mommy, Daddy, and her brothers were SWOOSHING through the roof too!

Mommy was holding Baby Jack. She looked around and saw Grandpa and Grandma. She saw some of her aunts and uncles too. All at once, they were standing on a cloud. In her dream Christy said, "I'm standing on a cloud!" She put her hands over her mouth and giggled.

Then she saw Him, dressed in white. Christy couldn't get over to Him, there were so many people. He took a step; she saw His face. It was Jesus! He was so beautiful! Christy blew Him kisses. Jesus smiled and waved. He looked so happy to see her.

Christy felt dizzy, like she was on a merry-go-round.

Everything was happening so fast.

She looked up at Daddy. He had tears in his eyes.

Christy knew why. Daddy's father had gone home to be with Jesus before she was born. Once Daddy had told her he missed his father every day. Now Daddy was going to see him again.

"Oh Daddy," Christy shouted, "I'm so happy! I get to see my other Grandpa."

Daddy picked her up and hugged her tightly.

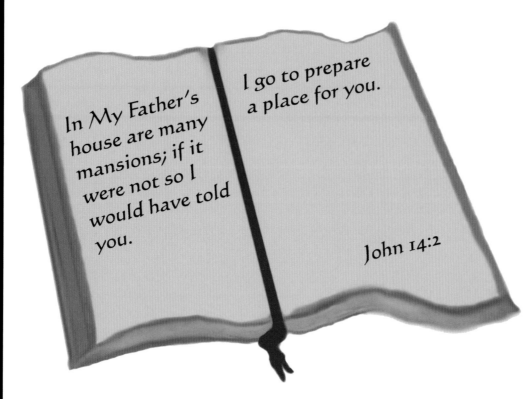

In My Father's house are many mansions; if it were not so I would have told you.

I go to prepare a place for you.

John 14:2

Before Christy could think again, a chariot pulled up. It was as big as a school bus.

A very tall angel was driving and he said, "All aboard. Next stop, New Jerusalem."

Mommy motioned for her to get on. Christy sat between Mommy and Raymond. Grandma and Grandpa sat across from her.

Suddenly she heard that SWOOSHING sound again! They were flying in a chariot, the wind in her hair.

Christy could see a light far away. They were flying very fast. As they got closer to the light, Christy could see they were coming to a city.

The city was clean, and bright and beautiful. All the houses were big! "Rich people must live there," Christy thought. (Read John 14:2)

The chariot stopped in front of the most beautiful house she had ever seen.

Christy could see through the window. There was a room piled high with toys. A clear blue river flowed through the back yard. Christy could see kids splashing and playing in the river. There was a big yard with a swing set, and flowers everywhere.

Mommy, Daddy and her brothers got out of the chariot. Suddenly Christy realized, "This is our house. It's so beautiful!"

21

Grandma and Grandpa got out, too. Christy was glad to see they lived next door.

The angel who drove the chariot spoke. He said there would be a big party soon, and they were the guests of honor. Jesus would be their host!

Just then, the bedroom door opened and Christy woke up.

Her goose down comforter had fallen on the floor. Grandma covered her up again and tucked the comforter tightly around her.

Christy was too tired to talk so she just turned over.

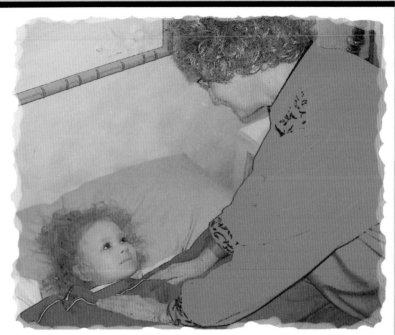

Before Grandma left the room, Christy was once again fast asleep.

Then we who are alive and remain shall be caught up... in the clouds to meet the Lord in the air. And thus, we shall always be with the Lord.

1 Thessalonians 4:17

NOT THE END

(READ 1 THESSALONIANS 4:17)

Only the beginning, it really is...
Happily Ever After!

Prayer of Dedication

Heavenly Father, thank You for sending Jesus to die on the cross for me.

Jesus, I love You. Come into my heart and I will live for You forever.

Holy Spirit, fill me to overflowing with Your love and power. Amen

Other books by Anne T. Garcia

From The Hidden

Desde el Escondido (Spanish version of From The Hidden)

From The Hidden
Box 494
Columbia, IL 62236